Like You and Me

For all children to perceive and admire the beauty of diversity.

Shahnaz Qayumi
Illustrated by: Shavon Cheng

AuthorHouse™
1663 Liberty Drive
Bloomington, IN 47403
www.authorhouse.com
Phone: 1 (800) 839-8640

Published by AuthorHouse 06/29/2020

ISBN: 978-1-4520-8397-1 (sc)
ISBN: 978-1-4772-0627-0 (e)

Print information available on the last page.

Library of Congress Control number:2010915472

authorHOUSE®

I will never forget that day. I was nine years old when a lady asked me, "Are you "Pashtun" or "Tajik"?

Pashtuns and Tajiks are the predominant ethnic groups in Afghanistan and yet I did not know which group I belonged to so I answered, "Afghan!"

I was puzzled with this strange question and, not knowing the concept of ethnicity, I rushed home to clarify this issue. I questioned my mother, "Am I Pashtun or Tajik?"

My mother demanded that I tell her what my response was to the lady who asked me the question about my ethnicity. Afghan! I repeated my answer to my mother. My mother peered deep into my curious eyes that were waiting for the right answer and responded, "You are absolutely right, you are an Afghan and nothing else".

This was an important lesson because it showed me at an early age that ethnicity does not determine who we are. Underneath all our beautiful diverse attributes we should be equally respected for being human.

My book, "Like You and Me", is a place for children to explore and celebrate the vast diversity in our world.

As an early childhood educator and a parent, I believe that we play a significant role in developing a sense of acceptance, appreciation, and love in our children. The earlier children are exposed to diversity in a positive light the more it will help them admire the beauty in every culture.

Children are not born prejudiced; I've known this since I was nine years old.

Far away from here

there are children like you and me,

but with a little bit of a difference.

They dress like you and me,

but with a little bit of a difference.

They wear shoes like you and me,

but with a little bit of a difference.

They eat like you and me,

but with a little bit of a difference.

They talk like you and me,

but with a little bit of a difference.

They sleep like you and me,

but with a little bit of a difference.

They respect elders like you and me,

but with a little bit of a difference.

They play like you and me,

but with a little bit of a difference.

See, they do everything like you and me, but with a little bit of a difference.

But you must know that they do a few things just like you and me.

They laugh like you and me.

They shout like you and me.

They cry like you and me

They love like you and me

They dream like you and me.

ABOUT THE AUTHER

Shahnaz Qayumi was born in Kabul, Afghanistan. After finishing high school in Kabul, she went to Kiev, Ukraine on a scholarship where she received her Bachelors and a Masters Degree in Developmental Psychology and Pedagogy.

In 1980, she returned to Afghanistan and started working as an Assistant Professor at the Department of Psychology of Kabul University. She was forced to flee Afghanistan with her family to Pakistan because of the brutal communist regime that captured power in Kabul. She served in refugee camps while living in Pakistan. She left Pakistan shortly after and immigrated to Canada.

After facing challenges such as language, cultural, and educational barriers, she was able to establish herself in Canadian academic circles. She has taught Early Childhood Development to the Native Education College, Kwantlen University College, and Vancouver Community College. She has facilitated an Early Childhood Education program for Family Empowerment funded by the Ministry of Health in North Delta for low-income families. She has also been a member of the Cultural Diversity & Ethnic Awareness committee, a member of Vancouver Women's Visible Minority, and also a Mentor in Leadership Roles in Canadian Society/National Organization of Immigrant and Visible Minority Women of Canada. She is a member of Canadian Women for Women of Afghanistan (CW4WA). In this capacity she has taught Human Development courses to trainers for a project called "Training the Trainers" in Kabul.

In 2005, due to interest and passion toward community work, she became a member of the Board of Directors of Partnership of Afghanistan (Canada) (PAC – a non-for-profit organization). In 2012, she became the Chief Operating Officer of PAC, and assumed the responsibility for building the Center of Excellence for Innovation and Research for Faculty of Psychology and Education at the Kabul University. She is also working to establishing a countrywide phone-based Parents Education system in Afghanistan. ♥

ABOUT THE ILLUSTATOR

Shavon (Hsiao-Fen) Cheng was born and raised in Kaohsiung, south of Taiwan. As a professional and proficient graphic designer, she worked for over ten years as an Art Director for an international advertising company in Taipei, Taiwan. Among her many works are illustrations for textbooks, magazines, and several advertising designs and publications. In 1991, her works were selected in Taiwan by DESIGNER PUBLISHER, INC. for a book titled TAIWAN CREATIVE GRAPHIC ARTS.

In addition to Like You and Me, Shavon has also provided illustrations for three other children's books, including Kokodiko (2004), Afsana Seesana (2014), and Zoe (2015).

Shavon now lives in North Delta, British Columbia, with her husband Glenn and her daughter Yuni. ♥

Printed in the United States
By Bookmasters